ENCOUNTER
ON
BURROWS
HILL

Athens, Oh

1968

ENCOUNTER
ON
BURROWS
HILL

AND OTHER POEMS

by

Conrad Hilberry

OHIO UNIVERSITY PRESS

For Marion

Acknowledgments

Grateful acknowledgment is made to the *Antioch Review* for permission to reprint "Three for Celia," "Encounter on Burrows Hill," "Train," and "Girl on a Bicycle"; to the *Beloit Poetry Journal* for permission to reprint "On Knocking a Huge Ant into the Fire," "Poet," "Gift on a Thirty-First Birthday," and "Hamster Cage"; to the *Carleton Miscellany* for permission to reprint "The Last Day" and "The Harrowing of Hell"; to The National Council of Teachers of English for permission to reprint the poem "To Robert Herrick" from the October 1959 issue of *College English* and the poem "Epigram" from the March 1962 issue; to *Epoch* for permission to reprint "Madrigal"; to the *Mad River Review* for permission to reprint "Fredrick Kouts" and "Love Poem"; to *The New Yorker* for permission to reprint "Hell-Diver"; to *Poem* for permission to reprint "Storm" and "Kick the Can"; to *Saturday Review* for permission to reprint "First Reader"; and to *Vortex* for permission to reprint "Mirrors," "Sirens," and "Chloe Courting Nelson."

I should like to thank Harper and Brothers for the Eugene Saxton Fellowship which permitted me to write some of these poems.

Contents

THREE

ONE

HAMSTER CAGE

Quiet, the children look on
As the small mammal
Nesting in chips and lettuce
Gives birth, bloody and natural.
They see how it's done,

Watch her licking them clean—
But more than licking, the teeth
Working on the diminutive head,
Back, haunch, one then both,
Till blood and a tuft of down

Make the only sign.
Drawn by cries, parents disbelieve,
Then, believing, go silent,
Send children off, remove
The unspeakable mother whose calm

Jaw mocked their bargain:
Treadmill, breadcrumbs, suet
In exchange for a clean bit
Of wilderness, a pet,
A cage of instruction.

THE LAST DAY

You know it when around the street's bend
Gorgeous
With garbage
The trucks move, end to end,

Leavings fermenting ripe and sweet,
Husk, rind,
Shell, bone,
Brown cabbage fragrant as meat.

And there on the running board rides a man
With cigar among molars,
Cocky as the moon,
His pail clanging like church-bells on the stinking van.

THE HARROWING OF HELL

Don't ask me. I was covering third
Looking to catch Gilkey in a steal
When Cortesi and Henschel began acting real
Twitchy and pointing at some bird
Flopping like a kid's kite over the east wall.
Pretty soon all over the yard the boys were
Prancing around like they got the itch or
St. Vitus Dance, for God's sake. Then this tall
Bastard, Hanson, and some of the rest got
To fanning and flapping like they planned to take off.
And damned if they didn't. Dangled their legs right off
The ground and hunched into the sky like a stringy lot
Of cranes.
           Not me. I'll sleep in this stinking cell
Till I die. Though God knows I flapped to beat hell.

TRAIN

The woods were already full when it blew
Its raucous coming. Forked
And open, trees stood in their bark,
The lake gave back the green
Of its shore; a muskrat knew

The savour of fur on its own hide,
And wood ducks made air
Heavy under their flight. Then far,
Its bray slapped the backs
Of trees in loud

Camaraderie. On it came
Parting the spruce
And wild strawberries, troubling mice,
Deer, fishermen trolling for pike,
Hallooing its simple name

As though no life moved but its own.
And then it rang
Upon us. My God, the charge of iron,
The tremor of earth. In an instant I rode
In the whale's eye, hand

On the whistle cord, the lunge
Of flesh under me—
Going someplace! But then gone. A spree,
A chance I did not take. Children
Stood silent; bathers at the lake's edge

Paused in the shallow water.
That enormous passage
Emptied fish of leap and plunge,
Birds of their tangled flight; even the trees
Whispered, "Yes, sir. Yes, sir."

GIFT ON A THIRTY-FIRST BIRTHDAY

Though comically the giver planned
The gift bow tie, blue dashed with gray,
I, who had gone four-in-hand,
Now sport the small bow every day.

And other fopperies ensue:
I wear plaid walking shorts for tennis
And ask my haberdasher's view
Of what the right beret for men is.

Already I begin to covet
A Volkswagen to drive to school in
Or better—indeed, far above it—
An Alfa Romeo to tool in.

What voice is it of summer ruth
Calls up the spurious, the sporty
And makes an unpretentious youth
Go gaudily toward forty?

AUGUST: THE PARK

Awkward and guileless
As a turkey
A boy roosts on a bench-
Back and smirks

At girls, his face homely and long,
His hair red
Like my own. Suddenly I perch
There in homebred

Agony, knowing myself a camel
Among mares.
Stupefied by the easy wit,
The bare shoulders,

I crack my knuckles
And grin,
Unable to leave, unable
To put in

One fitting word, a lumbering
Baserunner
Caught between hunger
And fear.

But the roost now is his
And I can say no spell
To charm him off that limb
Nor even tell

Whether a grace of words—
Smooth plumes
That soon may cover
His ungainliness—

Demands more honor
Than the turkey's
Grip, the long-faced grin,
This misery.

LOVE POEM

My spirit lay like U. S. 40 flat
And four-laned in the sun: six cylinders
Fired in time, and rubber withered past
A Dairy Queen, a blinker, a Marathon Station,
Following the tar line like a crayoned map.

Then in your topless car
You overtook me, honking
A musical horn, hair
Blown, fenders writing
Colors on the air.
My road curled like ribbon
And all my miles careened
Through breaking dusk, spun
In a field of meadow-rue,
And woke to the frivolous moon.

CEREMONIES

Two ceremonies grace the evening: Here
A brace of lovers gravitate toward bed;
There, the Sigma Deltas flower
Singing like tiger lilies on the quad.

While we practice in our skins, grotesque
As two recruits rejoicing that the Quarter
Master Corps can find no khaki
Cut to their civilian bone and butter,

The music promenades from grass to grass
In studied cadence, each part disciplined
To rise and fall to a harmonious close.
The girls applaud, invisible, behind

Their screens, and boys march homeward eight abreast
Down the narrow street, arms locked and voices swelled
With their accomplished rite. Having raised
Another sort of offering to the god,

An ancient gift, absurdly colorful,
We lie and wonder if that god is one,
That calls from blazered boys a musical
Salute and from us our rough devotions.

Or if we call by Love's name opposites,
One robed, cologned, who rides accompanied
By a troop of horse, and one who tumbles
By in motley, dancing and gesturing behind

The other's back. Which is clown, which sceptered
King? And which one animates the dreams
Of dormitory girls, assaulted
So melodiously in their dark rooms?

FIRST READER
IN A KIND OF MIRROR

(for Joe Galligan)

.kool, kciD, kooL
.pleh miT eeS
.krow miT eeS
.kool, hO

.god sih rof skool kciD
.god der emoC
.yalp, god, emoC

.yllaS rof skool kciD
.ynnuf skool yllaS
.yllaS, ynnuf, ynnuF

HELL-DIVER

"hell-diver, n. A dabchick or other small grebe."
     —*Webster's Collegiate Dictionary*

On the glebe
The small grebe,
Kin to the widgeon,
Moves with the gait
Of a celibate
Pigeon,
The tread
Of a scoter
Whose motor
Is dead—
He's a sick
Dabchick.

But afloat he is yare,
And steep as a merlin
Stoops in air
He drops through seas
That corals curl in,
Plummets,
The plumed, bizarre fish,
Headlong as though he's
Sighted a starfish
And aims to wive her,
The hell-diver.

STORM

"It's only thunder," we say, gelding the terror
With a name. The child goes back to bed,
And we, to atone for playing false with a god,
Go out to look at the weather.

From the porch—a sacred hollow behind
The waterfall—we watch the rain
Plunge from eaves, the spray gather and run
In the full pulse of the wind.

We duck together as daylight blooms
In the skeletal street and pales
With ghostly pollen the porches, the telephone poles;
Then liquid night dooms

Us again, though porch and pole still flash in our eyes
Like neon. Far clouds fork and flicker
And beyond our sight a low-voiced roar
Answers the sky's

Tongued eloquence. Awnings crack, the streetlight
Careens, blinking crazily,
Silver maples dodge and sway
In the exploding night.

Side by side we watch these dancers weave
An incantation out of sparks and spume
And find how willingly to this wild tune
Our civil bodies move.

OWL

The horned owl, Minerva's bird,
Blinks to see in a sunset wood
A muskrat furred
In crimson, a thin twist of red

Running where the black snake lies—
Every shape reworked in blood.
Two moons of eyes
Bloom innocent in his dark head.

Shouldering out his down-curved wings,
The bird, as readily as wind,
Drops through dusk and sinks
Cold talons in the rodent ground.

MARCH BIRTHDAY

Two starlings sail down
A wind, catapult
Above the crown
Of oak and elm, vault

Half the sky on headlong
Air, then suddenly
Swing
About and light on an ash tree.

So on my March day
I turn upwind and hang
And sway
A time to hear the clang

Of the sky's bell and watch
The low clouds ride, the willow
Weave and reach,
Bearing the year's first yellow.

The starlings and I
Mimic the redbird's song
But dry
Shrill, getting it wrong,

Perch, whistle awhile, then fling
Out, arch a down-wind way
On black wings
To celebrate a borning day.

FREDRICK KOUTS

Fredrick Kouts had not foreseen the seven
Dogs that followed as he walked his collie
Bitch in heat, a group so melancholy
He might have laughed to tell it, except that even

As he set out the seven moved too close,
Sidled up as insolent as beggars
Ramming confidences in his ears.
Their rancid backs and tails defiled his clothes.

With his wing-tipped shoes, Fredrick repelled
The spaniel, boxer, five mongrels, their mouths beady
With tongue and teeth, their instruments at ready;
And still they came till Fred's moustache curled

Like an eyebrow on his lip. In telling of it
Afterwards he said he took compassion
On the bitch's need, but she in the old fashion
Of queens ignored the commotion or reigned above it.

The boxer reared and mounted. Knit
To that working pick-a-back by a length of leash,
Fredrick looked away and made a phrase:
"Nature nodded when she did that bit."

Yelps, cries, an agony on the rope. He looked
And saw the last outrage: dog and bitch
Terribly linked tail to tail now, each
Pulling, one south, one north. Leash fallen, he walked

Smartly to his house, shut out the cries
And sat imagining how the bitch,
Now free, would foul herself in a stagnant ditch
Or hang perhaps from a limb by her flying leash.

T W O

CHLOE COURTING NELSON,
WHO STAMMERS

"That's all right Nelson, take your time.
The night's out walking, and the plum
Will lean on the porch till you can say it out.
Besides I like to watch your tongue
Arch and fight

Like a caught fish. The others pour such thin
Streams, it's good to see a turn
Of muscle there, even if it's stuck—
At least it doesn't skin
A rainbow slick

On the pond. Nelson, you know what
Your words do? They rise in your throat
And your Adam's apple punches them down
Like drowned kittens that float
Up and up again.

Kittens—or weasels, rats scratching
To be out? Apples bobbing
From wild water? Down them, Old Adam!
Slunk! Slunk! But still clamoring
To say their name

In the open. How come they sit
Right there in your throat? Mostly men silt
The beasts in at the bottom, safe
As bones—Snapper the old dog under the dirt—
Safe as a laugh

In the river mud. Nelson, I like
You; I won't care. Take the crick
Out of your throat and let words tumble
Like stuff over the dam: snakes,
Catfish, eels, windfall

Walnuts, a knot of weeds. Maybe
I'll stand below and catch the drench, debris
And sweet water together, cool
On the head. Or look, if I shake the tree
Words will fall

Like persimmons in November and mess us both up.
Here, a kiss. To draw the words. To suck
The staggering fruit. Dear Nelson!"
He held her while the plum breathed back
The easy run

Of wind in the night's throat and the river
Spilled its casual freight, leaves and litter,
Like seeds tossed over a shoulder. She
Waited. His lips, moving like water,
Spoke only, "Chloe."

MIRRORS

While tailor fingers at my neck
And measures intimately, crotch
To cuff, I study front and back
In triple view this patch

Of self—eyes spectacled, intent, nose
At point as though it sniffed advancement.
Chalk meticulously draws
The starting paunch, the chest, the slant

Of shoulders, while mirror within mirror
Diminishes a staring row
Of selves like decimals that wither
Mathematically into

Some farther room. Fitted, I leave
The triptych, pull on pants and braces,
Swing the revolving door and breathe
Again the sidewalk legs and faces

Past Gilmore's, Hoekstra's, Milton's Lunch.
Pretending now and then to glance
At rugs or medicines, I watch
A faint reflection in the glass.

MADRIGAL

All the green of the sycamore
And every myrtle's blue
Will fly as plovers do
South along the changing shore
To winter in a bay below
The fall of snow.

And light on water mottles still
As various as faces,
Shifts and lifts and laces
Day with webs of sun, until
Pell-mell as kingfisher in flight
Comes on the night.

So wise men's sons all go to school
To death's head, dust, and maggot
And learn how dry a faggot
This world is, and how the pool
Goes deep and empty in the bone
Where eyes once shone.

But while the knees can swing their weight,
While skull is still a world,
And the sweet dust swirled
Into a gesture and a gait,
I'll count the colors as love goes
In these bright clothes.

EPIGRAM

Acquainted with the bright young men
At Williams, Yale, and Wesleyan,
He speaks of Hal, whose books explore
The theory of metaphor,
George, whose *Collected Poems* is due,
Philip, the editor, and Hugh,
Who lives in Europe all the time
On a Prix de Rome or Guggenheim,
Recalls their ages, faces, gaits,
Their talk, their publication dates,
Then thinks on his own years, his fame
And drops another brilliant name.

TO A SATYR OVER THE ENTRANCE
TO THE BROADMORE HOTEL

I see you leer, tongue between teeth,
At the rich tan flesh that swings in underneath
You. Locked too long in that stone,
Your judgment cracks: if you should spring
Four-hooved from your architrave,
Breathe moist on her arm or touch her sleeve
With your alarming beard, do you
Imagine she would start like a doe,
Run barelegged over hills
Crying to the helpless rocks until
You overtook her limbs,
Her mouth? No, the nymph declines
To run. Instead, she pummels down
A fetid goat—stays long
Enough to see him tied and whipped—
Then in to lunch. Or else she slips
Into a hand carved chair
And runs a finger through his hair.

SIRENS

Like the distant crying of someone else's child,
Sirens rise and fall, urgent,
Across the dark city. Accident
Or arson, bad news speaks from this tangled
Whine. Yet to my ear the far howl
Comes in welcome as music on the night air.
Is it because it says flame still can stir
In the dry boards, peel plaster down, call
Out the trucks, the leaping-nets, the hoses
Flat on the street until they spring
With juice and issue a splendid Gulliver douse
To the wind? Or because, while flaming birds are
    whistling
Colors somewhere into the dark of windows,
In this house, for this hour, all fires are sleeping?

FRANCIS PASSMAN

In another life Judge Passman learned to march
In a rain forest, studied a way to slash
Clear the muscling vines, crouch through brush
And tilting trees, tolerate the itch
Of flies, webs bearding his face, the leech
At his leg; learned that over his boots the marsh
Would rise like reptiles if he stood in the lush
Moss unmoving. Or so I imagine, for each
Evening as he walks, his head ducks
From its tall place to dodge an invisible limb,
His feet shuffle a step from the sinking street.
Mosquitoes drink the deep blood of his neck
While his machete hand swings down to cut
And cut the sidewalk vines that seize him.

POET

"If the poet is tone-deaf as to sounds, it is best to rely upon
the phonetic symbols above each group of rhyming words in
the rhyming dictionary that terminates this book, or upon
dictionary markings. Many people can not distinguish the
obvious difference in sounds between this pair of words, which
do not rhyme:

NORTH, FORTH.

Take away the TH sound, and many people still hear no difference between this pair of words, which do not rhyme:

NOR, FORE.

Take away the R sound, and some people still hear no difference between this pair of words, which do not rhyme:

GNAW, FOE.

GNAW plus R plus TH can not rhyme with FOE plus R plus TH."
—CLEMENT WOOD, *The Complete Rhyming
Dictionary and Poet's Craft Book*

O, lucky poet tone-deaf
As to something else than sounds!
(Tone-deaf to the turning leaf?
Tone-deaf to autumn wounds?)

He walks in step with what he hears,
Keeps both beat and pitch;
Without a circumflex he fares
Foe plus *r* plus *th*.

This striding, compass-perfect poet
Never strays to *know-earth*.
Impeccably he sounds the note
And sets his foot to *gnaw-earth*.

GIRL ON A BICYCLE

Beneath her the spokes flick
Like a silent movie
And steady as summer weeks
The pedals rise
To the pull of her knees.

Down Xenia Avenue she rides.
Stately through shoppers,
Dogs and horns, she moves
Like water upright,
A wave that declines to break.

Then, two fingers to her teeth,
She blows a sweet
Blast that shivers the length
Of town, speaking fire or flood.
Cleaver, gas pump, coffee hot

From the urn, the whine of children—
Everything stops
But the thrust of her thighs,
Keeping their time,
The ready turn of wheels.

SURVIVOR

More than enough
Of hurricane weather.
Winds lie down long
Mornings with water
Welcome as dolphins now
But left leaves quiver
Wrenched heartwood when
A small air turns over.

TO ROBERT HERRICK

"*To his Book's end this last line he'd have plac't,*
Jocund his Muse was; but his Life was chast."
—*Robert Herrick*

Say Sapho and Corinna are but art
And Silvia imagined, every part;
Perenna's hair and Julia's thigh disclaim,
But never hope this truth will clear your name;
For zealous sects more readily excuse
An erring cleric than a jocund muse.

COUNTRY NIGHT

Locusts sang all night
Then in the hot
Wind that swung
On its neighing mane
All past-bedtime
Wonders: fireflies
Winking like one-eyed
Cats from cedar trees
And corn and trumpet vine,
Catchable cats turned
Torch in a mason jar,
And fireworks that burst
Like morning,
Flashing after
In your eyes,
Soda cold for fizzing
And no one noticing
We weren't in bed
As the lawn swing
Squeaked, bucked
On its haunches, and crashed
To grass while we hung on
And rode till the ground rose
And fell like an apple strung
From cedars or stars.

But I remember too
The bursting night bucked
Me back on my self,
Joys blinked

With cats' eyes timid
In the trees, and fear
Rode a fantastic horse
Whinnying dark as owls
Out of every shed and shadow
Of my city head.

KICK THE CAN

Crouching in the last light, I creep
By the rubbish drum and quake as if
This were no game, as if the sheriff
Would come with beagle hounds to leap

My name, as if all fences, driveways,
Alleys would point like witnesses
And old deceptions tongued with leaves
Would rustle out my hiding place.

Then darting, stopping, running back,
The keeper comes. I duck and hold
Till he's abreast of me, then bolt
Like a man caught in theft, weak

Knees crossing in flight, and catch the can
Full on the baked bean picture, send
It over-ending into the garden
And cry "All free, All free," the lawn

Buoying my sneakers, the evening street
Alive with prisoners escaping.
The keeper counts aloud. Leaping
The neighbors' sacred hedge, I sprint

For the lilac bush, squat to make me
Small, but for a moment scarcely care
If the give-away red of my hair
Blinks like morning out of the shrubbery.

THREE

THREE FOR CELIA

CELIA FIGURING

Celia, Celia, look away
If you should find me staring,
For double glances multiply
Like two's that fall to squaring.

CELIA AT TENNIS

Celia lobs a lovely ball
To treacherous mid-court,
Her backhand cross dispatches all
My cunning in the sport.

A glancing slam—she makes the shot
And has me forty-love.
She stretches, serves. What varied art
I am the victim of.

CELIA SPEAKS

For you, my Corydon, I carry
Coffee, like bowls of pomegranates,
Or like a letter on a tray
Conveying elegant regrets.

For you I tilt a bumbershoot
Across my shoulder, part a section
From an orange, stretch out a foot:
I study art in your reflection.

[47]

"Take care," they say, "the promenade
That starts in gardens ends someplace
Where beds are not so neatly made.
There smiles a satyr in his face."

But I, dear Corydon, contend
(Though doubting if it's well or worse)
Our shapely love will yet extend
Only to mirrors and to verse.

RIME

Pocket up the daisies,
Carry them for way's ease.
Ashes, ashes,
We all fall down.

Pluck the early apple
Where sweet and sour dapple.
Ashes, ashes,
We all fall down.

Crows and daws have eaten
Grapes before they sweeten.
Ashes, ashes,
We all fall down.

World can never steal all
The purple flower, the heal-all.
Ashes, ashes,
We all fall down.

ON KNOCKING A HUGE ANT
INTO THE FIRE

His look was black, unnatural, obscene,
But he would now live insolent and whole
Had I foreseen
His curl and wither on the coal.

SPRINKLERS: NORTH SHORE, CHICAGO

No vulgar spit and splash
Like sprung plumbing
Or an orange, jumped on;
No spume spiraling

Up like grasshoppers goosed
Into flight; no men on
Porches playing the spray on each
Peony equally, wetting down

The dusking grass with fond
Curve and stroke
Like currying a mare. In Glencoe,
Winnetka, and Skokie,

The turf dampens to the slow
Reach of deliberate thin
Streams, vaulting mathematically,
Like the pruned

Arc of elms, or like a row
Of real estate agents
Relieving themselves,
An ornament

To the suburbs.
Consider:
One could dome a plastic sky over
The whole North Shore,

Channel the cloudburst to
A gracious waterfall,
And remedy the rain's promiscuous
Pell mell.

ICE

When Coastguardsmen kept a lighthouse on North Manitou Island in Lake Michigan, they were often frozen in for several months in the winter. Sometimes, desperate for mail, they sawed the ice to get to open water and the mainland.

When sailors, bitter with wind, sawed
The tough bark,
Fought the freeze to the raw

Lake, what miracles did they expect
In the canvas pouch,
What letters like blue fields of forget-

Me-nots astonishing their winter
Landscape?
Or did they well enough foresee

Old issues of the Traverse City Star,
The Sears catalogue,
Mother's notes on a hard winter

With business slow at the store?
Did they foresee,
Yet know their need even for

Those dry bushes, those ungainly
Starlings to ease
The stillness of their gray country,

As we, sick for colors, watch
An auctioneer
Mumble brown pictures and cups, or stretch

To see bald Legionnaires limp in
The street and skinny
Girls strut and whistle the trumpets on,

Or gape at a warehouse fire, thirsting
For ladders, for sirens,
For huge smoke somersaulting
Like elephants over the splendid flames?

SIMILE FOR A GIRL

Like a boat loosed from the mooring's nuzzle
And jerk, from the reach of small water
At its throat, its stern's
Close pitch and yaw, she turns
To the deep puzzle

Of current—does not plumb it, rides
Instead on its slick skin
Unmanned, unruddered, kissing sand
Now, then swung by the stream, end
About, and on

Through brush, over the rise of logs,
Past the green streamers of willow.
Left at last in the hung drift
Of a bayou, she studies the gift
Of keel in low

Water, the just curve of her gunwales,
Feeds on the song
Of catbird, the blue turn of fish
In her shadow, indolent flesh
Of spring. Year-long

She sleeps in her own green before
Flood washes her back to the steep
Channel, to the wide mouth of water.
Year-long, where current brought her
But not in its keep,

She catches only the quick light
Of feathers, the fan of gills,
Turns all to shape and shadow, glass
To answer the furled poise,
The lift of her hull.

VARIATIONS ON A MADRIGAL THEME

A ha ha ha! this world doth passe,
Most merily, most merily Ile bee sworne,
For many an honest Indian Asse
Goes for a unicorne.
     Farra diddle diddle dyno,
     This is idle idle fyno.

II

Farra diddle diddle dyno
In the springtime blooms the thorn,
Young asses play the unicorn,
And grapes swell on the vine, oh.

Diddle dyno, idle fyno,
Now the mourning dove turns turtle,
Now sparrows in the myrtle
Tread berries into wine, oh.

III

Merrily, an honest ass
Put on a spiralled horn,
Neighed to the obedient woods,
And reigned—a unicorn.
He heard disputes among the beasts,

Flourished the royal quill,
Signed bills, proclaimed new feasting days—
And so he ruled, until
The animals complained of bray
Behind the royal nicker
And wondered if some lesser blood
Were mingled with his ichor.
"A fraud! A mountebank!" they howled,
"Lynch the unicorn!"
But quietly the ass reached up,
Took off the twisting horn,
And blew a long and whorling note
That spoke the wind's own name.
The beasts were still; then high and clean
An answering whinny came.
The forest moved; a white horse stood,
A spiral horn on his head.
He reared and flashed a royal mane,
Nickered again, and fled.
The ass took off the royal robes,
Put the quill away,
And walked alone into the wood
To find a wreath of bay.

IV

Aha, aha, the world still goes
Ripening from pose to pose:
Hear mockingbirds in every bush
Trade on the music of a thrush.

But what if the donkey should presume
To fleck himself with racehorse spume,
The gelding, sensing April blood,
Paw and whinny like a stud?

How can any gosling find
His habitat, his make, his kind
Until he tries the gay plumes on
And mocks the posture of a swan?

TO ROBERT HERRICK

Having prayed with Doctor Donne
In darkened chambers while the Son
Instructs his spouse, that sometime nun,
    In making holy love

And having tasted bread and wine
With Herbert in a windowed shrine
Where, with the twelve, men used to dine
    On God's own brooding Dove,

I walked a turn outside the wall
And found (though it was Devon) all
Was bright as spring and musical,
    And birds made glittering love.

Corinna stirred and met the May,
For matins went Aurora's way
Careless of dew in fields where lay
    The new green gown of love.

Julia shone as cherries do
Ripe in morning sun, and Prue,
Innocent of silks, withdrew
    To make the beds above.

Herrick, drive away the chill
Of indoor praise with music still
As graceful as the birds that fill
    The parish of your love.

CAROL

When April asks it, horses foal
And ewes drop lambs to earth,
Cattle ease the season's young
To fields green with birth:

Gently the creatures blink alive
To spring and all its gear—
But Mary lays her son on straw
The longest night of the year.

Ox and ass hoard up their warmth,
Shepherds freeze by a star,
Even kings must ride to find
Where their seasons are.

The fall has buried all its dead,
The day dropped under ground,
The sun lies dark, unless a child
Can turn the year around.

ENCOUNTER ON BURROWS HILL

Pedalling up Burrows hill, past Robby's Drive-In
And making it too, not getting off to walk it—
When a dusty grin
Comes wheeling from the top, spits
Gravel, bounces from pits

And chuck holes with the smack and slide
Of a boat topping water, his nose
Thrust like a mermaid
At the prow, a flag of my own colors
On his head. Passing he forks

Me a gesture, tosses the short end
Of a laugh, and spins by, legs straight
And strutting the wind
Now like yardarms, his tail taut
On the bucking seat,

Insolent as morning. I swing around
To follow him down, but he shoots West
        Michigan Ave.
Like a fool, full speed,
Nearly clipped by a pick-up truck, and banks off
Over the infield, through a grove

Of picknickers, still coasting high
As a drummer on horse, while the field tilts
Under his thighs,
The world all downhill to his spokes
As landscape slopes

Off in a dream. Out of sight. Gone. My shirt,
My voice—shrunk to that scrap of insect
Noise, that smirk
On the wind. Gone. Well, may God elect
To spill the cataract

Of his ride through gorges rattling with strange
     birds
Where rock and the cry of wind are bitten
To the shape of words
Speaking more ancient terrors than
Young fool and old, words sudden

As sun. And when he founders, wheels jammed
In a tree's fork, may the seed of the wreck spring
Whole to the untamed
Land: may he fetch from his tempered loin
The wretched mock of a son.